Renew Your Life Through Daily Devotions

Quality Time with God:
Book 1

Books by Paul J. Bucknell

Allowing the Bible to speak to our lives today!

- Overcoming Anxiety: Finding Peace, Discovering God
- Reaching Beyond Mediocrity: Faith's Triumph Over Temptation
- The Life Core: Discovering the Heart of Great Training
- Dying to Self: The Spiritual Discipline that Leads to Renewal
- Life in the Spirit! Experiencing the Fullness of Christ
- The Making of A Godly Leader: Isaiah 53, The Fourth Servant Song
- The Godly Man: When God Touches a Man's Life
- Redemption Through the Scriptures/ Study Guide
- Renew Your Life Through Daily Devotions: (Quality Time with God 1)
- Godly Beginnings for the Family
- Principles and Practices of Biblical Parenting
- Building a Great Marriage: Faith, Forgiveness, Friends
- The Lord Your Healer: Discover Him and Find...
- Christian Premarital Counseling Manual for Counselors
- Relational Discipleship: Cross Training
- A Biblical Perspective of Social Justice Issues
- A Spiritual Map for Unity: Break Through Impasses in the Church
- Running the Race: Overcoming Lusts
- The Bible Teaching Commentary on Genesis
- The Bible Teaching Commentary on Nehemiah
- The Bible Teaching Commentary on Romans
- Book of Romans: Bible Study Questions
- Book of Ephesians: Bible Studies
- Walking with Jesus: Abiding in Christ
- Inductive Bible Studies in Titus
- Life Transformation: A Monthly ... on Romans 12:9-21
- 1 Peter Bible Study Questions: Living in a Fallen World
- Satan's Four Stations: The Destroyer is Destroyed
- 3 X E Discipleship (Discipler and Disciple)
- Take Your Next Step into Ministry
- Training Leaders for Ministry
- Study Guide for Jonah: Understanding God's Heart
- Check out our Discipleship Digital Libraries at www.foundationsforfreedom.net

Renew Your Life Through Daily Devotions

Disciplines and Approach

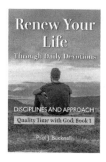

Quality Time with God

Series: Book 1

Paul J. Bucknell

Book Information

Renew Your Life Through Daily Devotions: Disciplines and Approach (Quality Time with God: Book 1)

Copyright © 2023 by Paul J. Bucknell
ISBN: 978-1-61993-113-8 (Paperback)

Also in e-book:
ISBN: 978-1-61993-112-1

The NASB version is used unless otherwise stated.
New American Standard Bible ©1960, 1995 used by permission, Lockman Foundation www.lockman.org.

Paul J. Bucknell, USA

Check out Paul's two websites filled with biblically-filled resources.

www.bffbible.org

www.foundationsforfreedom.net

Tribute

Our Amazing Father God loves to speak to each of His children, every believer, regularly and intimately! How patient and kind He, as the glorious Creator, daily listens to His humble creatures and strengthens them through His mighty Word.

With all my heart I have sought You;
Do not let me wander from Your commandments.

Your word I have treasured in my heart,
That I may not sin against You.

Blessed are You, O Lord;
Teach me Your statutes.

(Psalm 119:10-12)

Renew Your Life Through Daily Devotions

Quality Time with God: Book #1

An Introduction

Book #1: Renew Your Life Through
Daily Devotions

Biblical studies enrich
our personal devotional times with God.

I don't know when I first learned about devotions (daily time spent with God in prayer and Bible reading). Perhaps I learned backward. After I came to know the Lord at about thirteen years old, I didn't know about the spiritual discipline of reading God's Word daily, yet I instinctively wanted to read God's Word and pray.

This same desire drives Christians across the globe. A hunger for God's Word characterizes new believers. They hunger for God's Word like young infants long for milk.

This book will help you identify and describe your love for God's Word—or rediscover it. To be clear, to love God's Word doesn't mean you won't face issues reading it. To have questions about your time in God's Word is normal, especially if you are further along in your faith journey:

- Why don't I hunger for God's Word like before?

- Aren't I supposed to desire God's Word? What happened?

- Why don't I get much from God's Word anymore?

- How can I regain quiet times with the Lord like I had before?

Don't be shaken if one or more of these questions apply to you. They highlight needed spiritual adjustments and different periods of spiritual growth. Like our physical growth, we change spiritually too. I remember times as a parent when I finally understood how to care for a child at a certain stage, only to discover that he's suddenly outgrown that mindset and now requires a different parenting approach. Confusion is part of the growing process because unforeseen changes will inevitably occur.

Devotions, known by different names like quiet time, time with God, or morning/evening/daily devotions, is a crucial spiritual discipline for every believer. It is a time to meet with God in His Word and through prayer. Such activity typically includes reading and reflecting on God's Word and a time of prayer. Some people add worship songs, memorization, journaling thoughts or insights, and other spiritual activities like biblical meditation (dwelling on God's Word for further understanding).

My Excitement

I don't think anything has so radically changed my life as a regular quiet time with the Lord. Mind you, it's not the habit but what God does through the times while regularly meeting with Him. Like God's meeting with Adam (Gen 3:8) or Jesus with the Father (Matt 14:23), we should look forward to regular meetings with God.

This is why I am truly excited for you as you pursue God. We never know exactly where it will lead, except that knowing God through Christ is a wonderful, challenging, humbling, and eye-opening experience.

This is the first book in a three-book series designed to help you develop your relationship with God through personal devotional times. This first book explains what quality time with God (i.e., spiritual devotions) looks like and how days that start with inspiring times with God lead to renewal.

The second book will help us move beyond the discouraging traps that we tend to fall into, keeping us from growing in intimacy with God. The third book expands on the secrets God gives when we meditate on His Word and obey Him and how those insights tie in with our daily lives and help us live Holy Spirit–filled lives. (See Appendix 1 for further description of this series.)

Quality Time With God

 Book 1

 Book 2

 Book 3

Biblical studies that enriches one's personal devotion times with God.

Biblical studies that strengthens one's quiet times with God.

Biblical studies that shows how to use God's Word as a sword.

Rebuild foundations for renewal

Restore perspective for strength

Develop meditation for guidance

Preface

This devotional starter is not a cure-all. It is carefully designed instruction and Bible studies meant to renew your mind and spirit as you pursue God.

Many today ask questions about spirituality, wanting to know how to get closer to God. These studies provide insight and training and help you build a foundation for a strong, godly life.

We have admittedly kept this series brief, but it's because we believe that the foundation, though seemingly insignificant (i.e., daily quiet times), is enough to build a foundation for a lasting, strong spiritual life. The last chapter provides suggestions on continuing your walk with God.

Many Christians become confused and frustrated when they think about their spiritual lives. Don't let such thoughts put you off! First, identify your needs. The more specific you are, the better. Bring that particular need to the Lord in prayer. "Lord, this is where I am at. Please lead me to where you want me to be." A GPS app, ordinarily helpful in finding a path to our designation, can be terribly frustrating to those who don't input their present location or destination. This study guide aims to be a type of spiritual GPS you can use to help you find your location and clarify where you are going, thus providing your spiritual bearings.

Here are four categories of believers that can benefit from these studies.

New believers: These studies will help the new believer gain a sure footing in the Christian life. Although Christians are adept at leading people to Christ, very few know what to say after conversion. These studies can serve as guides to help new believers establish good and holy expectations in their relationship with the Lord. The studies unveil answers to the question, "What should the Christian life look like?"

Those fed up with stumbling: Some believers have known the Lord for a while but have fallen into some kind of sinful, critical, or doubting pit. And whether such a stage has lasted a week or ten years, the Spirit of God desires that you return to Him. These studies provide the reminders, guidelines, and hope needed from God's Word to get you back on track. Use this time to pursue the Lord. You will learn as you carry out the assignments. And although we do not focus on sin, it's critical to remember to repent from any sins. Indeed, it would be best if you did this before you begin or as often as a sin arises in your life. Aloud, confess all that you have done wrong and what you should have been doing. Ask the Lord to forgive you through Jesus' blood—His work on the cross, and guide you as you return to Him. He is waiting for you! This series provides an excellent combination of training, including Bible reading, examining His Word daily, example prayers, etc. But don't stop with this book—make sure you eventually move on to Book 2, which gives insight into how to keep from stumbling.

Those seeking renewal: These believers have known the Lord for years. These truths will not be new, though some may unexpectedly stand out, bringing fresh perspectives. We unknowingly fall into the snares of the evil one, which causes our spiritual lives to become routine and dull. For example, you can be sure that your faith has weakened when you consider devotions, going to church, prayer, or reading the Bible as boring. I don't mean that you are no longer saved—instead, your faith no longer properly shapes your life. The Lord seeks to draw you closer to Himself. This series can help renew your faith by providing you with tools to pursue Him better or even help others. Look to Him and use these studies to guide you to the goals He has for you.

"I'm not sure." Others might wonder why this study guide showed up in their life. Maybe God is using it to reground you in your relationship with Him. God is real and seeks your heart. If you wonder if it's worth it, consider Peter's response to Jesus: "Lord, to whom shall we go? You have words of eternal life" (John 6:68). The Lord is calling you to seek Him. Talk to the Lord honestly, "Lord, I'm not very interested in Your Word. I've been burned and lost interest. But if you are searching for my life and heart, please surround me with your hope and love, and lead me out of this stupor of faith." Wherever you find Him, follow His leading. If He speaks, listen and obey. Pursue God.

Guidelines for the Studies

Be regular. Seven daily studies combine short instructions with "Your Time With God." Take two or three days for each, as you please. For example, you can study part of the reading and look up the provided verses. But keep a regular schedule. Remember, one of the goals is to reconnect with the Lord so that you meet Him **daily**. See Appendix 3 for further thoughts on the reason for daily meetings with God. We also suggest using an extra day or two to look up and memorize the associated verses within a study.

Be honest. We do not want to pretend to be spiritual. The goal is to help you establish a firm foundation of faith built on the Lord (1 Cor 16:13). Many believers overlook their soul's dullness, assuming it's normal. They sometimes confuse their spiritual life with religious activities, falsely concluding they are the same thing. Tell the Lord exactly where you are at. (Appendix 2 includes more on Be Honest.)

Be expectant. Expect a unique, special relationship with the Lord—but don't demand how He develops it. God has uniquely placed and outfitted you—even if you feel very displaced at the moment (Isaiah 26:3). He often uses difficult situations to get your attention.

Look forward. Most of us are too preoccupied with our daily lives and need to spend time with God daily. The Lord wants to establish a long-term, growing relationship with each of us, but when we focus too narrowly on our feet (or our needs and the minutiae of life), we will stumble. We cannot progress if we don't know where we are going. To have a strong relationship with the Lord is to know where we are going.

A Lifetime Process

We have included a memory verse from God's Word with each day's study that helps develop a daily habit of reading and contemplating His Word in His presence. Memorization aids us in pondering His words.

Developing a strong devotional life is a lifelong process that brings fantastic rewards. You will better understand these meetings with God as we tackle one major issue at a time, providing a clearer view of a meaningful quiet time.

Go slowly through these studies. Don't hurry; take your time. This is a *process,* so be patient with your ups and downs and keep at it. Anticipate exciting times with God in the future! (A possible prayer: "I don't know what to expect, Lord, but keep teaching me how to live out each day of my life.")

Each study has an assignment. It's essential to work through each, including the small memorization work. Consistency makes it easier. My wife, for example, keeps a notebook to write down key verses and thoughts.

Each study has an area of focus essential to developing our relationship with God: connect, appreciate, hope, marvel, trust, discover, and expect.

Each of these seven aspects is a healthy relational criterion secured through faith in Jesus Christ and His Gospel.

Significant things happen when God Almighty meets with you.

Each trait is especially important for those raised in dysfunctional families who were never shown how to conduct good relationships properly.[1] Each aspect also can train us to work with other believers and encourage them in their daily time with God.

Enjoy your time with your Lord—the One who sits over the universe and time!

---

[1] My book, Relational Disciple, includes much more specific training for developing good, wholesome, godly relationships with God and others.

Day 1: Your Relationship with God

Connect

God's people greatly depend on His Word; God speaks, and they hear. Renewal happens when they discover the ways He uses His Word in their lives.

T he practice of daily devotions presumes a relationship with God. No one naturally has a good relationship with God. We are born sinners and enemies of God: "While we were yet sinners, Christ died for us" (Rom 5:6-10). God saves us through our repentance and faith in Christ's work on the cross, which initiates a new relationship between God and us. The Lord reconciles (literally makes peace with) us to Himself.

Spiritual Life and God's Word

This relationship with God is the result of the new life that God our Father has birthed in us through His Holy Spirit (Rom 5:5; Eph 1:13). Peter instructs us on how God's Spirit uses His Word to make us Christians: "You have been born again not of seed which is perishable but imperishable" (1 Peter 1:23). "Born again" speaks of our spiritual birth (John 3:3).

The Word of God plays a vital role in finding and developing our spiritual lives. The "living and enduring word of God" continues to work in each genuine believer (1 Peter 1:23). How amazing!

The Desire for God's Word

Peter uses the intriguing image of birth and a baby's instinctive desire for milk as a spiritual analogy.

> Like newborn babies, long for the pure milk of the word, so that by it you may grow in respect to salvation. (1 Peter 2:2)

As new babies hunger for milk, new believers are spiritually hungry for God's Word. It is a blessing that He gives us this desire for "the pure milk of the Word," upon which the welfare of our spiritual growth depends.

God uses this longing to usher us into a closer relationship with Him through which He bears spiritual fruit in us.

The Discovery

God is our Father, the Giver of physical and spiritual life, and I am increasingly amazed that He has made us His children. I love how John puts it: "But as many as received Him, to them

He gave the right to become children of God, even to those who believe in His name" (John 1:12).[2]

Identifying that the new believer's initial interest in reading God's Word originates in and follows their restoration to God is helpful. Our reading does not earn this relationship, no matter how thorough or regular. We are saved by God's grace, not by our efforts—even if that effort is to read the Bible.

Reconciliation with God through Christ brings us from the barren world into His magnificent presence!

Never conclude that your salvation—your newfound relationship with God—is due to keeping this or another devotional habit. This is a lie that distorts the facts. You are a child of God by faith in Jesus and His work on the cross, not through your obedience to spiritual disciplines.

Identifying Our Interest in God's Word

Our relationship with God develops as the Word of God nurtures our faith. Our faith is strengthened as we connect

---

[2] New Life - John 1:12-13 Study Questions & Answers: https://bffbible.org/d1/view/life-john-1.12-13-questions

our interest in God's Word (and the willingness to obey) with God's way of cultivating our relationship with Him through His Word. His Word increasingly becomes a priority to each growing Christian.

Thank the Lord whenever you notice this desire for His Word—it signifies God's remarkable work in your life. Daily quiet times build assurance of God's desire to "speak" to us through His Word, which builds up our faith. His Word is your spiritual food, so naturally, you ought to change your lifestyle to prioritize meeting with God each day in His Word. It sustains you.

You want to know Him more, and He welcomes you to deepen this relationship with Him. "Draw near to God and He will draw near to you" (James 4:8). God calls us all to step deeper and deeper into the depth of His love. Your new birth assures you of the Holy Spirit's ongoing work in you (John 3:6-8; Phil 1:6).

A Few Extra Thoughts

You might be wondering about those times when you feel no spark of interest in God's Word. We will address this later in this book as well as in Book 2. Those dry times are indicative of spiritual struggles. It's essential to think of past or present moments when God used His Word to comfort, lead, or otherwise help you. Did He give you hope? Did He move you by reminding you how He sent Jesus to die for you? Did

He use one of His promises in His Word to keep you steady on His path?

We often don't realize how God uses His Word to grow us throughout our lives. Of course, it's easy to forget what God has done, falsely concluding that God never "speaks" to you. He has, of course, and we need not let the evil one so easily take away our hope and faith.

Some believers might notice an increased thirst for God's Word at points in their lives. These times mark a unique work of God's Spirit, reviving His people on their long spiritual journeys. Like a tide that lifts all the boats, the Spirit of God heightens each believer's relationship with God at these times. But just as our newfound thirst for God's Word at our spiritual birth will fade, these special times of renewal in our journeys will also fade—but this recession allows us to consciously develop our relationship with the Lord.

Connect

We affirm that we belong to God by embracing our need and desire for His Word, which God daily uses to draw us closer to Himself.

Study 1: Your Relationship with God

- Memorize and study 1 Peter 2:2. What characterizes a new believer's life? (I've used the NASB Bible version; see Appendix 2 for more on Bible versions.)

- Think back on a few times when you desired God's Word. Thank God for a new life in Christ that gives you the desire to know His Word.

- Write or record your story of getting to know God through faith in Christ. If you are still determining if you are a Christian, check out Appendix 2.

- Peter states that your longing for His Word has a greater goal: "you may grow." Watch the Lord as He leads you through this growing process. List two ways He has led or grown you recently.
  Note: Never question your salvation experience just because you've missed a devotional time or find that you are not as hungry for God's Word as before.

- Observe how your desire for His Word has fluctuated throughout your Christian life. How would you describe that desire for His Word now? Ask Him now to help you grow more. Be honest in your conversation with the Lord.

- As God leads, spend an extra day reviewing the Bible references in this chapter to see how they support and teach various truths.

Summary

Our desire or thirst for God's Word is a natural outflow of our spiritual relationship with God—but sometimes, the desire fluctuates. Don't worry. Remember that God seeks to grow your relationship with Him each day primarily through the Holy Spirit's use of His Word to connect with and work in you. Identify where your desire is now and ask the Lord to give you regularity and intimacy, a goal we should all continually seek. Spend time with Him each day, even if only for a short time.

Day 2: Your Friendship with God

Appreciate

When we note God's steps to befriend us, we can let our guard down, initiate honest, prayerful conversations, and explore our growing relationship with Him.

Your regular times with God should become a daily spiritual discipline that helps you know God better. Good devotional times are like a great conversation between friends. From your experience, what are three or four things that are conducive to fostering a deep friendship?

God uses the same things to develop our relationship with Him. This might sound strange because God is great, and we are only humans.

But God demonstrated His own love for us by sending His Son Jesus to die for our sins (Rom 5:8). That is something He has already done for us, but it begs the question: why would He want to save us?

He saved us not only to give us eternal life but to restore the ability to develop a wonderful relationship with Him. God, not a mere force but a powerful, invisible person, created us in His image so that we might know Him and work alongside Him. It's not wrong to think of this relationship with God as a friendship. We all, deep down, want a friend with whom we can share our deepest joys and problems. Jesus is that Friend! He says:

> 13 Greater love has no one than this, that one lay down his life for his **friends**. 14 You are **My friends** if you do what I command you. 15 No longer do I call you slaves, for the slave does not know what his master is doing; but **I have called you friends**, for all things that I have heard from My Father I have made known to you. (John 15:13-15)

Devotional times are opportunities for intimacy with our Friend. Of course, we need to love Him as our Savior and respect our Lord as our Creator. Jesus expects us to obey Him (v. 14). However, God hopes a budding friendship will grow within that understanding. If we continue to respect Him, we can, like Joshua, Moses, and others, increasingly enjoy a growing and blessed relationship with Him (Joshua 1:7).

The best friendships do not develop when one person does all the talking. We don't listen much when we're preoccupied with our lives. We're only interested in information that provides input to what immediately dominates our minds and feelings.

However, to have a good friendship with God, we need to unhurriedly, like Mary, listen to our Lord as we daily reflect on His Word (Luke 10:39-40). Admittedly, many situations and seasons in life can interfere with seeking Him, but that is the topic of focus in book two of this series.

Appreciate

Our friendship with God strengthens our trust in His good purposes for our lives.

Study 2: Your Friendship with God

- Review John 15:13-15. Pick at least one verse that stands out to you and memorize it. Review the verse you memorized from chapter one too.

- Have you ever thought of your friendship with God as one of the reasons He saved you? Why might He desire a friendship with you?

- Have you ever considered Jesus, now risen from the dead, as your Friend? How do you usually think of Him (Matt 28:20)?

- Your admiration of the Lord deepens as you ponder His kind intentions. How has He shown His love for you? Thank Him now for each way.

- Why do you think it can be hard to develop stronger friendships? Think about how this might affect your relationship with God.

- Identify at least two characteristics of a good friendship. How are they applicable to your relationship with God?

- Thank the Lord for His intentions of drawing you into a deeper relationship with Him. Pray for one or more areas where you can improve your friendship with the Lord.

Summary

God died for us to rescue us from bearing the judgment our sin deserves and present us spotless before God, making us His close friends. Our devotional times serve as a crucial means to develop that friendship. When we regularly meet with God, we deepen our friendship with Him, which enables us to work with Him for His grand purposes.

Day 3: Your Life with God

Hope

Hope flourishes when we discover God's commitment to patiently work for our good—His commitment to us brings a fantastic amount of focus and motivation.

The strength of our desire to know God better and understand His thoughts is evident by the consistency in reading His Word. God typically quietly reveals Himself and His purposes as we read His Word, gradually building up our faith. He converses with us through this process. Part of our spiritual growth is characterized by the degree to which we "hear" Him. We don't typically hear His voice through our ears but through the godly thoughts that He brings to mind. Like Samuel, we often don't even realize God is speaking (1 Sam 3:6)!

Spiritual growth often happens in spurts—the same way we develop from babies to young adults. As we master the ability to apply spiritual truth to our lives, our spiritual growth will stabilize, leading to fewer ups and downs. What we learn when we are young can enormously influence our lives, perhaps because we are more impressionable.

The spiritual maturing process should continue throughout your life. This vital truth keeps you from becoming spiritually stagnant at one or more points in your lives and simultaneously conveys confidence and hope on several levels. We see five of these hope principles in Philippians 1:6.

> For I am confident of this very thing, that He who began a good work in you will perfect it until the day of Christ Jesus. (Phil 1:6)

Five Principles of Hope

First, God "**began a good work in you.**" He is growing you. He gives you spiritual life, which brings hunger for His Word and spiritual growth, which is characterized by good works.

Second, this hope keeps you focused. Instead of becoming complacent or distracted, you wonder what the next step of spiritual life will bring. How will He "**perfect it**"?

Hope comes from God's commitment to work in you.

Third, you won't easily think that God has abandoned you when you weather trials. You will gain hope from His work in you, being "**confident of this very thing.**"

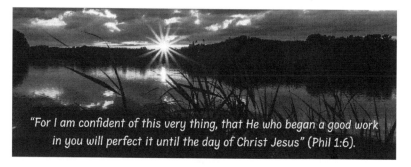

"For I am confident of this very thing, that He who began a good work in you will perfect it until the day of Christ Jesus" (Phil 1:6).

"He who began a good work in you will perfect it until the day of Christ Jesus" (Phil 1:6).

Fourth, the Lord keeps us focused on **His** work in us rather than on our own works, steering us away from legalism: "**He who began** a good work in you." Obedience remains important, but it's not what earns us our salvation. Full satisfaction of God's righteous judgment occurred because of Jesus' work on the cross (1 John 2:1-2). We are unworthy of this saving work in us, but because of His amazing work in us, we can grow in our delight to be His.

Fifth, you can expect to enjoy your walk with God **"until the day of Christ Jesus."** Yes, there are many things to learn in the journey, but as you grow, you will improve your ability to associate His work in your life with what happens around you. God is in control, and you are glad He is! "Bless the LORD, O my soul!" (Psalm 103:22)

His work in us follows our new birth, delivering on His promise of hope for the future, even as we follow His leading in our lives.

Hope

The Christian's knowledge of God's patient work in his life helps him understand spiritual development as a series of steps rather than a one-time experience.

Study 3: Your Life with God

- Are you generally a hopeful person? Explain. What makes you most hopeful?

- Memorize Philippians 1:6.

- Have you ever considered your spiritual life as God's good work in you? Explain the meaning of "good work." What is He trying to do in you and me?

- Of the five truths listed in Philippians 1:6, which means the most to you? Explain why. As time allows, choose the second most meaningful principle.

- Why is confidence in God's work in you so crucial? What most easily shakes your confidence?

- What are one or two character traits that the Lord is developing in you right now? Pray for this process now.

Summary

Hope is a crucial aspect of your Christian life and growth. **Hope comes from God's commitment to work in you.** Our hope grows stronger as we observe God's steady work in us. What He started, He continues until Christ comes! No exceptions.

Day 4: Your Encounters with God

Marvel

God uses our quality time with Him to prepare us for our daily journeys, where we can further discover how He works in our lives.

God is genuinely remarkable. We will spend all our lives and eternity getting to know Him and His wonders. Our many encounters with God during regular devotional times will gradually transform our lives and make us more like Jesus (Gal 4:19).

There are no limits to deepening our relationship with Christ nor are there cautions against spending too much time with Him. The Scriptures often use the word "blessed" or "grace" to describe the many benefits of knowing God.

I've been a Christian for over fifty years, and I've maintained these devotional times for most of my Christian life. Instead of being repetitive, they have become my most rewarding and challenging moments.

Psalm 89:15-16 opens our eyes to the special relationship God desires to have with His people.

> 15 How blessed are the people who know the joyful sound! O Lord, they walk in the light of Your countenance. 16 In Your name they rejoice all the day, and by Your righteousness they are exalted. (Psalm 89:15-16)

The phrase **"walk in the light of Your countenance"** describes how engaged we should be in our relationships with God. A relationship with God has many amazing effects.

Try to pinpoint at least one thing that could result from walking in God's countenance (i.e., His presence) as described in the above verses. For example, consider how God might use His Word to spur you on during your exchange of thoughts with Him. Observe how He helps you through what you are learning, what happens when you spend time in His presence, or how He imperceptibly increases your faith and love. Delight on how the Lord refreshes you through times together.

God regularly teaches us about life through His Word. In this sense, we can say our devotions are an opportunity for purposeful time spent delighting in His countenance. The phrase **"They walk"** suggests how they, and we, too, remember His presence throughout the day.

We need to be aware of God when reading His Word—it is His Word, after all! We can keep our minds inquisitive as we search for Him: "What are you trying to teach me today, Lord?"

"Walk in the light of Your countenance."

He teaches us how to live in light of His presence throughout the day. Far from being a legalistic tool, the command to "Pray without ceasing" is a lifeline to the Lord (1 Thes 5:17). Learn how to say aloud (or write down) your honest prayers to God throughout the day, expressing what is on your heart and what you're dealing with in life, including the ups and downs.

We spend time memorizing God's Word because we want to remember what He spoke to us later in the day as we're going about our business. Having verses at the front of our minds increases our awareness of His presence and reminds us of what He impressed on our minds early in the day.

Our encounters with God

Mind-boggling

Mysterious

Magnificent

Marvelous

Devotions become a daily routine to get you started in your day-to-day relationship with God rather than something you must do or finish. It's a beginning. For this reason, I suggest you train yourself to have a morning quiet time before you get engaged in the web, check your phone, or take on life's many activities. Also, plan your night routine to accommodate your time with God the following morning. Start with brief devotional times. Even ten minutes is good to get you started. Keep this time as unrushed as possible, however long it lasts.[3]

When you look at your time with God as a time of preparation for your journey with Him through the day, you will find that God increasingly shapes your life.

---

[3] I love a believers' zeal when they excitedly commit to reading 30 to 60 minutes a day, but it's better to start with a less demanding schedule and slowly increase. Not many can live up to their initial excitement. If you have extra excitement, do an additional study on top of your regular quiet time.

Marvel

Christ's disciples walked closely with the Lord, learning to interpret their circumstances and serve others.

Study 4: Your Encounters with God

- How would meeting a famous person like a president affect you?

- Would meeting God in your quiet time have the same effect? Why or why not?

- Memorize Psalm 89:15-16.

- Carefully read Psalm 89:15-16 and note everything that results from walking "in the light of Your countenance."

- What results characterize your walk in God's presence?

- Do you reflect on God's presence throughout the day? Why or why not?

- What step can you take to better reflect on God's presence?

- Do you think it's fair to describe morning devotions as a time to start your day with God? Refer to: "O Lord, they walk in the light of Your countenance."

Summary

Quiet times are not just a brief period you check off your to-do list. They are purposeful meetings with Him (no matter the length) that help you live in light of His person and purpose throughout your day!

Day 5: Your Pursuit of God

Trust

Spiritual struggles like the dullness of the soul reveal our need for a Savior, prompting us to apply our faith and pursue His grace to overcome.

An intriguing event occurred for a widow in Elisha's day (2 Kings 4:1-7). Her husband, a prophet, died, and her two sons would be sold off to pay their debt. However, Elisha told her to get as many empty jars as possible. Somehow, God would supernaturally fill them from her one jar of oil. She could sell the oil to pay her debts and live on the rest. It was a fantastic miracle demonstrating God's special care for His servants, but it also illustrates the need for faith.

How much oil did she pour out? The amount she received depended on how many jars she collected. So, how many jars did she gather? How many would you collect if you were in her situation?

Part of the answer concerns how many jars were readily available. No problem. But how far would she search for empty jars? It became a test of her faith. The oil stopped when the last empty jar was filled.

We get as much as we seek. Jesus speaks of this Biblical truth, "Ask, and it will be given to you; seek, and you will find; knock, and it will be opened to you" (Matt 7:7).

This Bible verse has much to do with our quality time with God in His Word.

Daily rediscover God's love and care—and thank Him!

About three or four times a week, I feel rather dull about meeting with God and reading His Word—though I don't always realize this is the case at first. Spiritual dullness drives down our interest in His Word, challenges our pursuit of God, and threatens to undo our time together.

One sign of a dull soul is when I don't even bother to bring one "empty jar" to my meeting with God. I frankly don't think I need Him and His Word. How preposterous!

Although we depend deeply on God, we often forget Him and ignore our genuine need for Him. Comfortable lives condition us to forget His extended grace and favor and to fall into spiritual lethargy.

How conscious we are of our need for Him is a gauge of how much the Lord will bless our devotional times. Even though I know how much I need God—and have even written a book on it—I still need to work through the dullness of my heart! It is such a common problem.

God doesn't want us "to just do" our reading of His Word as a habit; He desires that we seek these encounters with Him, our living God. But how do we reactivate our faith?

Reflecting on Our Needs

We first must **detect our lack of faith** by observing how we don't care much about our times with Him. I might think more about a sports game or meeting up with my friend than conversing with the One who made the earth. It's ridiculous, but it happens! As I said, we bring no jars for Him to fill. The dense spiritual fog begins to break up when we cultivate awareness of our great need for Him.

Second, **don't be afraid** of your cold heart. The evil one has somehow clogged your spiritual sensitivities. This spiritual unawareness doesn't mean the truth is unreal. The devil has snuck in and mucked up your spiritual sight, which greatly affects your feelings and expectations (Eph 6:11).

Third, disperse your dense spiritual gloom by **honestly observing** where you are at and telling the Lord about your situation in honest prayer. Here's a sample prayer:

"Wow, I don't know why my heart is so dull today, but I need you so much, Lord! I can't even function this day without You. You are great! Radiate your grace in my life. Teach me through your Word!"[4]

In this prayer, we start by confessing our dull hearts, which reminds us of God's amazing love and stirs up some small gratefulness in our hearts for what He does for us. We then rediscover how reliant we are on Him and seek Him to fill the empty jars we bring to our time together. He might fill those jars with forgiveness of sin or with encouragement from a near disaster yesterday.

As we ask, seek, and even knock, we come to Him in need, and He kindly pours His grace on us. Our hearts become grateful as we watch Him patiently care for us.

I often check on my desire for His Word by asking myself whether I really want to read God's Word. I further expose my "need level" by asking myself how much I need His Word. More often than not, I need to confess that I don't feel I need His Word. I should realize how much I need to rely on the Lord, but somehow my true needs for God are blacked out.

There is a mysterious association between our pursuit of God and the blessings we receive. Our pursuit depends on how aware we are of our need for God. Our reward depends not on time spent but on our expectations and faith.

---

[4] I provide further training for this in, "Reaching Beyond Mediocrity: Faith's Triumph Over Temptation." https://www.foundationsforfreedom.net/Help/Store/Intros/Reaching-Beyond.html

How many empty jars do you bring today for Him to fill? How much do you desire that He teach you?

Trust

Spiritual struggles are active war zones that require pursuing God in faith, and seeking His abounding grace for all our needs.

Study 5: Your Pursuit of God

- Read 2 Kings 4:1-7. What do you think is God's primary purpose for recording this event? What was the sequence of events?

- How many empty jars would you get if you were in the same situation? Why? What would your attitude be if you were her?

- List five things you depend upon God. Are you good at remembering your need for Him? Each need becomes a place where God can make Himself known to you.

- Have you noticed that your heart is spiritually dry? How do you respond when this happens?

- Memorize Matthew 7:7. How does this theme of dependence relate to quality devotional times?

- How can you instantly break out from dry devotional times? Glean hints from above.

Summary

God's Word comes alive when we regularly take time to cultivate an awareness of our needs before God. However, the evil one attempts to muffle our spiritual sensitivities. We pursue God by being attentive to our needs and expressing them in honest prayers. We pursue our faith-based relationship with God, digging out from spiritual lulls by His grace.[5]

---

[5] This teaching is further developed in the second and third books in this series.

Day 6: Your Understanding of God

Discover

God sprinkles unique circumstances in our lives to reveal His glory, dismiss our many wrong assumptions, and grow in our admiration of Him.

W e greatly need our Lord's grace. However, our discovery of God's excellence must go beyond how He cares for us. We must allow Him to break our stereotyped belief of who He is.

It's a little like a friend who visited the Grand Canyon, a place you've never been to and want to know more about. So you ask your friend, "How was it?" It's hard for your friend to describe because it's a place that an individual needs to experience personally.

Because God is eternal, there will always be much to learn about Him (Psalm 61:2), despite how much we've learned!

One key to this learning is not allowing our wrong assumptions of God to take away from our desire to know Him. Here are some common false assumptions about God that distort our view and minimize our faith in Him (Ex 20:3-4)[6]:

- We expect God to fulfill our every need, which causes us to treat Him as our servant rather than our Master.

- We believe the most significant world is the one we see and are unwilling to open our lives to the greater spiritual world where He reveals Himself (Eph 6:12).

- We blindly treat our will as the definitive answer, trying to control or manipulate God, though He remains the unmovable Sovereign God.

- We think God is surprised by what is happening in the world, but God already knows everything from the beginning to the end. He is Sovereign.

- Life isn't about getting what we think is best but learning how God uses life's circumstances to train us to be mature and serve others.

Wrong concepts of God hold us back from deepening our relationships with Him. For example, we might go to Him only when we need something, and, for the most part, that is the only time we talk to Him. Our faith (what we believe), be it big or small, shapes our relationship with the Lord.

---

[6] All these distortions of God become forms of idolatry. Today's modern or postmodern philosophies make an individual's life their focus, making them the idols, a sort of "me-ism."

Our faith can only grow as much as we invest in getting to know God better. This growth is best viewed as "steps" in our faith. Often, such growth occurs through challenging situations—I'll call them faith-demanding times—when God expands our understanding of Him.

After the ten plagues and the destruction of the Egyptian army who attempted to pursue the Israelites across the sea, Moses and all of Israel sang a song in Exodus 15.

> 1 Then Moses and the sons of Israel sang this song to the Lord, and said, "I will sing to the LORD, for He is highly exalted; The horse and its rider He has hurled into the sea. 2 "The LORD is my strength and song, And He has become my salvation; This is my God, and I will praise Him; My father's God, and I will extol Him. 3 The LORD is a warrior; The LORD is His name." (Ex 15:1-3)

Our experiences are not so astonishing, but Moses' written words, which are God's words to us, teach us something remarkable about God. Let me point out one observation.

Worship arises when we connect the wonders around us with the greatness of our Lord. Moses announces, "**I will sing to the LORD**" (1). The picture of God's excellent ways became more apparent to Moses through everything that happened in the Israelites' exodus from Egypt. He connected awesome things with the LORD's doing, "**The LORD is His name**" (3).[7]

---

7 His name LORD, Yahweh (Jehovah), is written in all capitals in some English translations, like the NASB and ESV.

Our spiritual lives grow when we can connect the many small yet significant events in our lives to God's ways. Examples of the small things that point to God include His creation, His special work in us, and provision for daily life. God increasingly becomes our God. We learn who He is by identifying how He gets involved in our daily lives, thus strengthening our relationship with Him through events and His Word. Our studies of His Word open our understanding of how He uses events to teach us.

Discover

God launches us into the deep waters of life so that we can discover who He is. Get ready for the journey ahead!

Study 6: Your Understanding of God

- What are one or two wrong assumptions you have about God? (Use the list above if helpful.)

- How do misunderstandings about God negatively influence your faith in Him?

- Memorize Exodus 15:2.

- Go through Exodus 15:1-3 and find all the descriptions about God. (Read slowly through the passage several times.)

- Share with a person one real-life experience that God used to open your eyes to His great ways. (Write it down if no one is nearby.)

- What is one difficult situation that you are facing right now? Ask Him to teach you about Himself through it. Keep track over time of how He answers your prayer.

Summary

We develop false understandings of God because of certain underlying assumptions we make. But God patiently breaks these down as we spend time with Him in His Word and become more familiar with the truth of who He is.

Day 7: Your Excitement in God

Expect

When we observe how He uses our quiet times to bless, reward, and lead our lives, the expectations we have for our daily meetings with Him rise.

My wife used to hide prizes throughout the house for scavenger hunts on special occasions like birthdays. Our kids would scramble about eagerly, hunting for treasures! I remember how they used to scurry back to base when they could find nothing else but then rush back out once they heard there were one or two more hidden treasures.

The quality and regularity of your devotional times are directly related to how much you expect to find. Are you expecting anything from these meetings with God? If so, what do you expect to gain? If not, why do you think nothing fruitful will come of your time with God?

Our eagerness to meet with God is of utmost importance. You are fortunate if you have friends who also have a morning quiet time. (It's okay for the night owls to have evening devotions, but they ought to be conducted as looking forward to the next day, reviewing what you learned earlier that day to apply for the new day.) Ultimately, your motivation must come from **the reward of meeting with God.**

> And without faith it is impossible to please Him, for he who comes to God must believe that He is and that He is a rewarder of those who seek Him. (Heb 11:6)

Hebrews 11 links the faith of past saints with their pursuit of Him, the living God. They rightly believed God closely observed their search for Him and rewarded their efforts.

Admittedly, you will not always sense an immediate reward (Heb 11:13). The process is much more subtle. This is where the self-discipline and faith of this spiritual discipline come in.

Holding a daily time with God gets you into gear while everything slowly comes into focus. For example, you might be tired from not sleeping well or worried about a test that day. This can interfere with your fellowship with God. You need an honest prayer to set your mind right. Below I've included two example prayers you can utilize for such times.

> Lord, I didn't sleep well last night, but I'm here. I need you. I suppose I need you more than if I slept well. I tend to look at everything negatively when I don't sleep well. Will you

help me get beyond my tiredness and find one or two
people I can help today?

———————————

Lord, I didn't realize that I was so worried about today's test
until I tried to read your Word. I wasn't thinking about your
Word as I read it—I was distracted by the possible test
questions. Forgive me. I have so much to learn. The test will
come and go, but You are my eternal God. You are worthy
of all my heart, mind, and strength. Please show me how to
live above worry. I know I have a long way to go, but show
me step by step.

These prayers should, in time, come naturally to you—not
only during devotions but throughout the day. You are not
trying to impress God with your prayers but are honestly
speaking to Him about your situations and needs. Such
prayers transform tough times into stepping stones that help
you gain a better glimpse of how God helps you through
your days. Part of the reward is the extra grace that enables
you to be more loving and gain deeper insight, patience, or
help.

You can trudge through your devotions without faith and
gain nothing, or you can use an honest prayer to connect
with Him and gain the faith you need for the day. It makes a
huge difference.

Do you meet the Lord in His Word regularly? Why? Have
you ever realized that spending that time can lead to a reward
for you? An expectation of a reward is not selfish but wise!

The faith hidden in this expectation is just what God wants to see in you. Your belief in Him drives you to meet with Him! Or, on the contrary, you don't meet with Him because you lack faith and don't expect much help from Him.

The evil one constantly baits us with false conclusions and attractive false promises, but God wants to equip us to do our best! Quality time with God becomes special spiritual workouts where He subtly, and sometimes very powerfully, prepares us for a Christ-filled life.

Expect

Our spiritual growth takes off when we see how He actively intervenes in our lives to bless us.

Study 7: Your Excitement in God

- List a few things you are motivated to do. Why?

- Do you believe God will richly reward your time in His Word? Why or why not?

- Memorize Hebrew 11:6 and review the verses you've already memorized.

- List at least three rewards the Lord might give someone who seeks Him.

- How is faith connected to pursuing Him?

- Share a problem you are facing and how He might reward or further equip you to face that situation properly, bringing more thanks to Him.

Summary

A believer's expectation of finding rewards from the Lord becomes his daily test, revealing how closely his faith relates to what profit he gets from the Word. We are thankful that an honest prayer brings us wayward ones quickly back on track!

Finding Your Next Step

After finishing this book, you might ask, "What's next? Where do I go now?" Those are great questions! I wouldn't want someone to lead me into the forest part-way and then tell me to find the remaining way on my own!

These studies are foundational because they set in place certain truths that will guide you in your ongoing quest to know the Lord.

The guidance from these studies will cease, but the Lord's presence will never depart from you. Jesus told His disciples, "And lo, I am with you always, even to the end of the age" (Matt 28:20).

There is no need to rush to the second book in this series. Give yourself some time to enjoy simply meeting with the Lord regularly. Establish a good spiritual routine of reading God's Word, confessing sins, having honest prayer, growing in one's faith, and having good conversations with the Lord. Note what problems you face along the way, but don't let them hold you back from meeting with Him.

When the time is right, move on to the next book.

- Book 2 can help you overcome obstacles while maintaining quality time with God. This is a spiritual battle!

- Book 3 elaborates on how to better conduct your studies in God's Word by unlocking biblical meditation's mysteries and revealing how God involves Himself in your daily life.

Helpful Hints!

A right perspective. Don't equate your spiritual life with church life. Church life is necessary but builds upon your relationship with the Lord, not vice versa. Daily time with God refocuses our lives, even if we feel dull in our meetings with the Lord.

Live in faith. Start each day by rejoicing in the Lord's presence, no matter your feelings or circumstances! This often needs to be done in faith, for we don't feel like doing it. His great love is the backdrop to our lives, encouraging us to be persistent in developing our relationships with Him. There is no more faithful friend than our Lord.

A challenge. Stay in His Word. One way to do this is to find a list of promises from God's Word. Take a Bible promise each day and ask Him how He tries to shape your expectations of Him and life through that promise (2 Peter 1:3-4). (I just briefly searched and found this online page with fifty promises.[8]) Keep considering why He, the mighty God and Creator, would promise you anything good.

Keep it up! After compiling these promises, read through the Psalms or shorter Bible books. Try reading a paragraph or chapter at a time, but pick out one significant verse from your reading. See why that one word or verse might stand out to you. Some websites provide a verse a day. Journal your thoughts with Him. Be careful not to get distracted by what others say (including this book), though it be good. Train your spirit to learn from the Holy Spirit's illumination of God's Word (John 14:26).

Take note. Be aware of what pulls you away from your relationship with the Lord. For example, it might be a late-night movie or an argument. The Lord is testing whether you want to meet with Him or play a video game. Confess your sin as needed. Shift your priorities to keep the Lord first. The Lord will reward you.

Never fumble. It's okay to get confused, not understand the Bible passage before you, or not know what to ask Him. There are many things you might experience as you read God's word. Sheep are like this; that's why we need our Good Shepherd (John 10:11)! But don't let confusion or difficulties overly trouble you; stay confident in God! Keep talking to the Lord about your situations and thoughts. Your honest prayers keep you connected to the Lord. Talk to Him

---

[8] Fifty Promises: https://www.biblestudytools.com/topical-verses/gods-promises-verses-in-the-bible/

about what you are facing, how you handle it (maybe good or bad), what you need, etc. Let your spiritual response be like your physical one. If you stumble, the rest of your body instantly moves to lessen the impact of or avert any potential fall. God is always there, so rely on Him and talk with Him about everything, even your missteps!

Enjoy. Focus on enjoying your relationship with the Lord. Our journeys of faith continue, learning more of His Word and integrating your life with His, but He's always there to assist you. He wants you to win.

I hope this list helps you continue your walk with the Lord through the forest of life! Check out Appendix 1 to better understand the purpose of Books 2 and 3.

Appendix 1:
About This Series

Quality Time with God

Getting to know God is the beginning of a lifelong relationship with Him.

The three books comprising *Quality Time with God* are designed sequentially to teach you how to approach spiritual life to grow in your relationship with the Lord.

Book 1: Renew Your Life through Daily Devotions

* Disciplines and Approach

Quality Time with God, Book 1 builds on the initial love God's children have for His Word. In seven studies, believers learn how to regularly meet with God using seven essential steps to know and encounter God: connect, appreciate, hope, marvel, trust, discover, and expect.

You will learn how to initiate real-to-life expectations of God in your spiritual lives through brief readings and embed this spiritual discipline in your lives through daily exercises.

Book 2: Restore Confidence for Ongoing Devotions

* Difficulties and Delight

Book 2 instructs believers on handling obstacles they may face when trying to have quality time with the Lord. We try hard, but problem after problem often deter us from our objective of maintaining those quality times with God. We can move beyond these issues by God's grace to find rich fellowship with the Lord.

As we work through these issues, we can persistently grow in the Lord, becoming much more aware of how the evil one attempts to impede our spiritual growth. Meanwhile, we seek the Lord and, through Him and His Word, regain perspective, hope, purity, and joy in the Lord. He's so patient and wants us to succeed.

Book 3: Reveal the Power of Biblical Meditation

* Deeper and Closer

I will share numerous aspects of effective biblical meditation resulting from an intense encounter with God. Studying God's Word integrates God, His will, and life lessons into our lives. Invite Christ to fully live His purposes through you and learn how to explore His Word deeper. He's alive and seeks to work through us as we abide in Him.

Appendix 2: Simple Answers about the Christian Life

Bible versions

There are many English Bible versions. All are acceptable, but some are better to memorize and study from—like the more literal NASB (which we use) or the increasingly popular ESV version.[9] Others are more readable and helpful to understand a particular passage but do not replace a regular study Bible. Maybe these easy-reading Bibles can be likened to the "pure milk of the word," suitable for beginners but not as beneficial once one's teeth have come in and are ready to "chew" the meat of God's Word. For more, read Choosing the Right Bible Version.[10]

Assurance: "I'm not sure I'm a Christian."

Many Christians question their faith, asking, "Am I a genuine believer?" It's best to focus on the now than the past. Do you presently believe Jesus is your Savior? Do you follow Him and ask Him to lead you? Do you sense a need for a Savior, a God who loves, forgives, and cares for you?

---

[9] Beware of Bibles and books that cults use. Jehovah Witnesses have their poor translation, "New World Translation."

[10] Choosing the Right Bible Version by Paul J. Bucknell. https://www.foundationsforfreedom.net/Topics/Bible/Bible_Version.html

The unbeliever does not have this inner desire for God's Word. If you do not long for God's Word, I encourage you to follow Jesus Christ (click for more).[11]

Be honest.

I've regularly used this phrase, be honest, to emphasize its importance to spiritual growth. Being honest about one's life is similar to confession. "If we confess our sins, He is faithful and righteous to forgive us our sins and to cleanse us from all unrighteousness" (1 John 1:9).

Some Christians sometimes vaguely say to each other that they are okay or good. This is completely unhelpful. This passive communication can contaminate our prayer lives and induce a phony, shallow relationship.

To be honest requires you to search your life to see the present status of your soul, whether bad or good. Start there. Openly tell the Lord what's on your mind.

Don't merely say what God wants you to say, "I'm a sinner" or "I try to be good." Instead, tell Him the specific ways you sin, doubt, don't trust Him, etc. Here's a sample confession: "You probably didn't want me taking that money yesterday or watching this TV show tonight." In Book 2 we will provide a few reasons why half-honest spiritual self-assessments keep us in the dark.

---

[11] *Born again to a new life.* www.foundationsforfreedom.net/Topics/Belief/GainingNewLife.html

Tell the truth about how desperate or good your spiritual life is. Your feelings, thoughts, attitudes, and choices reveal much about where you are at. Being honest is a sign of God's work in you (John 3:19-21)!

Appendix 3: Historical Insights

Old books on godly living are rare. I'll provide insights from two resources: Calvin's Rules of Prayer and Lewis Bayly's suggestions for effective Bible reading.

Calvin's Rules of Prayer

Calvin had five rules of prayer that can give us insights into the honest prayer I speak above,[12] but I will refer to the church historian's summary below.[13]

(1) The first rule is reverence...This is how we come into prayer, recognizing who God is, being in reverence of him, and in light of him, recognizing who we are.

(2) The second rule of prayer, and that is that we pray out of insufficiency.

(3) The third rule is that we come pleading mercy. We don't deserve anything.

(4) Calvin's fourth rule for praying right is that we pray with confident hope.

---

[12] Calvin's Institutes, Book 3, Chapter 20. https://ccel.org/ccel/calvin/institutes.v.xxi.html

[13] Calvin on Prayer by Stephen Nichols. https://www.ligonier.org/podcasts/5-minutes-in-church-history-with-stephen-nichols/98-calvin-on-prayer

(5) The fifth rule is that we pray in Jesus' name. Jesus is our intercessor, our mediator.

The honest prayer that I mention openly confesses our failures and needs. These needs awaken our souls and draw us again to God. Our big struggle is that we are not regularly aware of our daily needs. Jesus teaches us in the Lord's Prayer, which John Calvin made his lengthy comments, how to pray for these genuine needs (Mat 6:11-13).

Lewis Bayly on Effective Bible reading

The Practice of Piety: A Puritan Devotional Manual (taken from 1842) by Lewis Bailey, pp. 105-106.

How to Read the Holy Scriptures with Ease, Profit, and Reverence

"First read a chapter in the word of God; then meditate awhile with thyself, how many excellent things thou canst remember out of it.

First, what good counsels or exhortations to good works and to holy life.

Secondly, what threatenings of judgments against such and such a sin; and what fearful examples of God's punishment or vengeance upon such and such sinners.

Thirdly, what blessings God promiseth to patience, chastity, mercy, alms-deeds, zeal in his service, charity, faith and trust in God, and such like Christian virtues.

Fourthly, what gracious deliverance God hath wrought and what special blessings he hath bestowed upon them who his true and zealous servants.

Fifthly, apply these things to thine own heart...as if they were so many letters or epistles sent down from God out of heaven to thee.

Sixthly, read them, therefore, with that reverence as if God himself stood by, and spake these words to thee...

Appendix 4: Are Daily Times Necessary?

What do the Scriptures indicate about meeting with the Lord each day?

Many wonder why I push daily meetings with the Lord. This discipline best builds up our Christian lives and fellowship with the Lord. Every time we meet with God, He brings extra benefits to our lives that we wouldn't otherwise possess.

First, note the Psalmist's focus on his **daily** experiences:

> But his delight is in the law of the Lord, And in His law he meditates day and night. (Psalm 1:2)

The mandate leads us into an encounter with God each day through His Word. (The Psalmist mentions several times in a day—day and night.) Today, we have the convenience of personal copies of the Bible and the ability to read it, though admittedly, it can still be challenging to understand.

Two Analogies

Let's now look at two common analogies, eating and sleeping, that we can use to illustrate why we ought to meet with the Lord daily.

God likens spiritual hunger to a baby's desire for milk. This analogy highlights our appetites, which seek fulfillment every day, multiple times a day (Matt 4:4). We might eat well one day, but this doesn't make us not hungry the next. The Lord likens spiritual bread to physical food, both of which strengthen our lives. Even without further explanation, this analogy should inspire us to meet with the Lord daily.

Our nightly need for sleep should have us draw the same conclusion. Sleep closes each day, even as our awakening ushers in a new one. In Matthew 6, Jesus told us to treat each day as its own. "So do not worry about tomorrow; for tomorrow will care for itself. Each day has enough trouble of its own" (Matt 6:34; see also 6:11; Eph 4:26). Jesus suggests that sufficient grace will be given daily to us. In the same way, we need the Lord's daily strength and guidance.

Reasons for Quiet Times

Though the above two analogies instruct us on the necessity of daily meetings with the Lord, they don't explain the critical reasons for regularity. Here are three: (1) spiritual edification (lit. building up), (2) increased help that results from our growing friendship with God, and (3) eternal rewards.

(1) **Spiritual edification.** The Christian who wages spiritual war (Eph 6:12) requires daily spiritual strength from God's Word to fight and discern (i.e., light) how to stand protected, carrying out God's will. "Finally, be strong in the Lord and in the strength of His might..." (Eph 6:10).

(2) Increased help. A good friend is someone with whom you regularly connect, share difficult struggles and situations, and gain further insights and companionship. The Lord remains our best friend, staying with us even when others are not. I've stressed how important it is to express daily honest prayers with the Lord as a way to grow in that friendship. You will increasingly admire Him as you stay close to Him.

(3) Eternal rewards. Each day presents further opportunities to express our dependence and delight in the Lord. Our eternal rewards are based on how we live here on earth. The Lord seeks to increase those rewards (John 15:16). A new day comes with new opportunities to draw close to God, pursue Him, confess our sins, and assert His faithfulness to carry out His appointed good works and glory in His Name. The apostle says, "I die daily" (1 Cor 15:31). Making a life commitment is good, but the daily exercise and recommitment to live in light of God's truth and love are what provide an abounding life.

Summary

We can get by without eating a meal and squeeze by without meeting with the Lord today, but why? Enjoy the best of life by regularly meeting with the Lord! Make it part of your daily experience. Don't feel boxed in, though; learn to be mindful of Jesus Christ daily as you live! Explore life with Him and what He teaches you daily. In Book 3, we will learn how to commune with Him through biblical meditation daily.

Appendix 5: More on the Author

Paul J. Bucknell

Paul worked as an overseas church planter during the 1980s and pastored in America during the 1990s. God called him to establish *Biblical Foundations for Freedom* (BFF) in 2000. Since then, he has been actively writing, holding international Christian leadership training seminars, and serving in the local church.

Paul's wide range of biblically based books and media-rich training materials on Christian life, discipleship, godly living, leadership training, marriage, parenting, anxiety, Old and New Testament studies, and other spiritual life topics provide many practical insights.

Paul has been married for more than forty beautiful years. With eight children and eight grandchildren, Paul and his wife Linda always watch God's blessings unfold.

➡ Check online for more information on Paul and Linda and the BFF ministry.[14]

➡ Or check out his two websites under BFF.

www.bffbible.org

www.foundationsforfreedom.net

---

[14] https://www.foundationsforfreedom.net/Help/AboutBFF/Biography.html

Appendix 6:
<u>Your Notes</u>

Appendix 7:
About This Book

Renew Your Life Through Daily Devotions:
Disciplines and Approach
Series: Quality Time with God — Book 1

This is the first of three books written to help us develop our relationships with God through personal devotions. God designed us to work with Him through life and teaches us how to keep a good relationship with Him, providing perspective and godly motivation. These seven studies on renewal supply the critical building blocks for a growing relationship with the Lord.

Day 1: Connect
Your Relationship with God

God's people greatly depend on His Word; God speaks, and they hear. Renewal comes by freshly discovering ways He uses His Word in their lives.

Day 2: Appreciate
Your Friendship with God

When we note God's steps to befriend us, we can let our guard down, initiate honest, prayerful conversations, and explore our growing relationship with Him.

Day 3: Hope
Your Life with God

Hope flourishes when we discover God's commitment to work for our good patiently—His commitment to us brings a fantastic amount of focus and motivation.

Day 4: Marvel
Your Encounters with God

God uses quality time with Him to prepare us for our daily journeys, where we further discover His beautiful ways of working in our lives.

Day 5: Trust
Your Pursuit of God

Spiritual struggles like the dullness of the soul reveal our need for a Savior, prompting us to apply our faith and pursue His grace to overcome.

Day 6: Discover
Your Understanding of God

God sprinkles unique circumstances in our lives to reveal His glory, dismiss our many wrong assumptions, and grow in our admiration of Him.

Day 7: Expect
Your Excitement in God

When we become aware of how He uses our quiet times with Him to bless, reward, and lead our lives, we build the expectations of our daily meetings with Him.

Made in the USA
Columbia, SC
07 October 2024

43220080R00054